FIZZ

Barbara Serulus &
Elise van Iterson

INTRODUCTION

I received my first scoby (symbiotic culture of bacteria and yeast) for my 30th birthday and I was overcome with excitement. This was a familiar feeling: it arises each time I'm convinced that something (an encounter with an awesome person, a new article of clothing, a book or an amazing shampoo) will change my life profoundly or even shake the foundations of my very existence. Later that evening, I mused about all the good that would come my way. In my mind's eye, my life was divided into two eras: before scoby and after scoby. Because, if all went well, nothing would ever be the same.

In the meantime, I've fortunately become a bit more realistic; yet, in a sense, the prediction did come true. My life did change because, from that moment on, fermented drinks have had me under their spell. I set to work with the kombucha scoby using the copied instructions that came with it. When I'd managed to keep my scoby alive for a year, I went looking for water kefir grains. And so, the fermentation jars began to spread throughout my house.

For a long time, because I thought I should keep this obscure hobby to myself, I was careful not to talk about it too much. Gradually, though, people started asking me more and more questions about my fermented brews. In all sorts of roundabout ways, strangers in search of a scoby found their way to me, friends asked if they could make the drinks themselves, and restaurants were interested in putting them on their menus. Since so many people were looking for a healthy alternative to soft drinks or wanted to give up alcohol temporarily or for good, the interest in these naturally fizzy drinks kept growing. And that is how I came to write this book about them. I hope my enthusiasm is infectious and that, after reading this book, you too will start to experiment with the knowledge that I've picked up in recent years. Don't worry if it doesn't always work out: after all, fermentation is a natural process that at times — just like you — dares to be quirky.

Fizz

Fermentation produces fantastic non-alcoholic drinks: imagine a refreshingly tart kombucha, a thirst-quenching water kefir or an earthy beet kvass, each with a complex and surprising taste and fizz due to their healthy bacteria. They are showing up more and more in restaurants and cocktail bars — but you can easily make them yourself. With their natural effervescence and slightly yeasty flavour, fermented drinks are a fine alternative to wine or beer. Ideal for anyone wanting to consume less alcohol and give their body a probiotic boost.

This book tells you everything you need to know to brew these healthy, alcohol-free beverages yourself. We show you that it's not complicated at all to start fermenting. And we guarantee that by the time you have finished this book, your house will be full of jars gently fizzing and bubbling.

In the following chapters you'll find user-friendly recipes with step-by-step illustrations, bite-sized nuggets on the science of the fermentation process, and juicy anecdotes about the origin of these remarkable drinks.

What is fermentation?

Fermentation is the process whereby bacteria, moulds and yeasts are utilised to transform foods. A fresh head of cabbage becomes sauerkraut; a sweet 'soup' of grain becomes a potent, bubbling beer; a soft cheese ripens to become an aromatic flavour powerhouse. These magical processes unfold without human intervention. All we can do is watch in admiration and, even then, we don't see much: the action takes place at the microbiological level. These days scientists peer down their microscopes to examine lactic acid bacteria and sourdough yeasts thriving in petri dishes; but for centuries, humans have relied on intuition in their attempts to master this elixir with trial and error — or in other words by smelling, tasting, and spitting it out again.

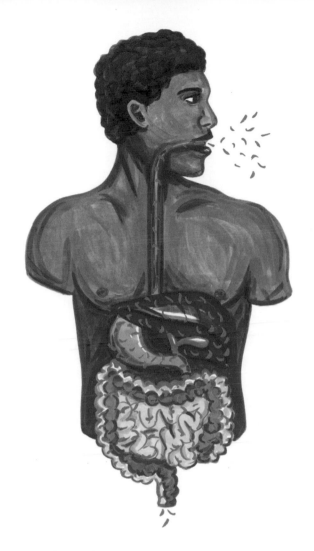

Why ferment?

Fermented foods and drinks contain masses of microorganisms. These useful little beasties give foodstuffs a more robust flavour, a longer shelf life, and a different texture. They are also beneficial to our health, able to provide extra vitamins, convert sugars to organic acids, and break down ingredients which are difficult to digest.

Why is fermentation good for you?

In our passion for hygiene, Westerners have declared war on bacteria. But guess what? It turns out that banning bacteria from our lives has harmful effects on our immunity. From an early age, our immune system needs exposure to microorganisms to learn to recognise organisms that cause disease and to stop an immune response once it has done its job. In recent decades, contact with microorganisms in our environment has decreased drastically: we have little contact with animals, soil, and plants. And industrialisation has led to our food being more sterile than ever.

Because there are millions of bacteria in fermented foods, consuming them is a good way to get back in touch with our old friends, helpful bacteria. In our bacteria-shy lives, fermented foods can contribute to our resilience.

More and more scientific studies are providing evidence for the connection between our brain and our gut. For example, a healthy microbiome — the ecosystem of bacteria in your intestines — has been linked to good mental health. Most of our hormones are produced by intestinal bacteria and since hormones such as dopamine, noradrenaline and serotonin are instrumental in promoting feelings of well-being, it's no wonder that researchers are looking with zeal at combatting depression with probiotics.

Take probiotics or drink kombucha?

The microbe species found in fermented foods are closely related to the species marketed as probiotics. Probiotics are microorganisms selected as a result of various scientific studies that have demonstrated their health-promoting properties. Still, the probiotics currently on the market will never be as diverse as the mix found in spontaneously fermented foods — and this diversity is crucial to a healthy gut ecosystem. Instead of swallowing pills, then, you can sip a small glass of kombucha, kefir, or kvass.

Save the culture

As you start fermenting foods you might be surprised by a heady feeling of power. You are, after all, single-handedly creating something. The shift from consumer to producer can feel gratifying in a society in which our place is usually at the end of the supply chain. Moreover, you will be keeping centuries-old yeast and bacteria cultures alive, thereby helping to sustain our culinary culture.

Wild and cultivated fermentation

When you rely on the wild yeasts and bacteria found on vegetable and fruit peels or floating in the air, we call that wild fermentation. This spontaneous process leads to the creation of an incredibly local product, alive with organisms from your specific environment. This is true for ginger beer, mead and tepache, and you will find recipes for these drinks in this book.

Another form of fermentation uses cultures. These combinations of yeasts and bacteria have come into being at some point and are passed down from one generation to the next in the form of scobys (symbiotic cultures of bacteria and yeast) such as the mushroom-like disc that floats on kombucha or the grains used to make kefir. Cultures are also produced by adding a small amount of fermented product to the next batch, as with a sourdough starter or yoghurt.

Non-alcoholic

We have termed the majority of the drinks in this book 'non-alcoholic' or 'alcohol-free'. We use this label because these fermented brews rarely contain more than 0.5% alcohol, which is the upper limit according to current European law. Keep in mind that where you live — regulations vary from country to country — fermented drinks may not be considered alcohol-free, since the fermentation process always produces some alcohol. And if you're after a 0.0% thirst-quencher, then fermented drinks are not for you.

Practical matters

You won't need any expensive or special materials for the recipes in this book. The things you do need, and need to know, are listed below.

Glass jars

Fermenting drinks works well in glass jars. You can see what is going on through the glass, and glass jars can be cleaned thoroughly and do not react with the acids that develop in the liquid. The size of the jars depends on the amount of beverage. If you want to brew large batches, keep an eye out for a glass bottle of the type called a demijohn or carboy, as these can hold up to forty litres.

Metal containers are not recommended because the acid in the fermented drinks can react with the metal. Although stainless steel could be a solution to that problem, common household items are often coated with only a thin (and therefore easy to damage) coating of stainless steel.

Glass bottles

After the fermentation phase, it's best to bottle your drinks in glass bottles that can be sealed tightly so that the CO_2 can't escape and the drinks will be fizzy. Examples include glass preserving jars or recycled water bottles with screw-on tops that close tightly. Plastic bottles would also be possible except that the acids in the liquid can lead to reactions that you would rather avoid.

After bottling, watch very carefully for pressure build-up in the bottles. In warm temperatures, lots of CO_2 — and thus pressure — can develop. Keep an eye on your bottles and open them now and again to check how much gas the bottles contain. To stop the fermentation, put the bottles in the fridge. Don't fill your bottles right to the rim: if you leave room for the CO_2 you'll avoid exploding bottles.

For safety's sake, open your bottles above a mixing bowl placed in the sink. That way you can catch the drink if it happens to foam out of the bottle like champagne. To avoid a repeat performance, reduce the length of time you leave the bottles to ferment outside the refrigerator.

Other tools

You also need:

— a funnel for pouring the liquid into the bottle
— a sieve to strain the liquid to remove herbs or other flavourings
— a clean (cheese)cloth or piece of paper towel to cover the jars with
— a kitchen scale to weigh ingredients

Hygiene

Always use clean glass jars and bottles for fermentation. We only want the good bacteria to grow in our drinks; working with clean materials keeps potential disease-causing bacteria at bay. To get the jars and bottles really clean, rinse them with a mixture of water and vinegar.

Water

For fermentation, it's best to use filtered water. The chlorine in tap water, added as a disinfectant to kill harmful bacteria, can also prevent the growth of good bacteria in your fermentations. But you can use tap water if the recipe involves boiling it to make tea, as for ginger beer or kombucha: the boiling process causes the chlorine to evaporate.

Ideal conditions

Always cover your fermenting liquids so that no dust or flies end up in them. If you live in a cold climate, put your brews in a warm place such as the kitchen. Never put them in direct sunlight.

1 KOMBUCHA

The origins of kombucha are shrouded in legend. It is said that Chinese Emperor Qin Shi Huangdi, who reigned over 2000 years ago, was one of the first fans of kombucha. The story goes that the emperor ordered his troops to round up all the doctors in his realm. After imprisoning them, he commanded the doctors to compile a list of all remedies for the most common ailments. When they had completed the task, the emperor asked the assembled physicians to choose one remedy from the list that would guarantee him a long life. The wise ones were unanimous: it had to be kombucha, the tea mushroom culture that holds the promise of eternal life.

FOR STARTERS

Kombucha is a sweetened tea that starts to ferment when you add to it a specific combination of bacteria and yeast. To the naked eye the bacteria and yeast colony looks like a flat, white rubbery mushroom, floating on top of the tea. The technical name for this is 'scoby', which is short for 'symbiotic colony of bacteria and yeast'. The scoby converts the sugar in the tea into CO_2, organic acids, and vitamins. From ancient China to today's health-food circles, people have attributed superpowers to this drink, although no conclusive scientific evidence backs up the claims about its detoxifying effects.

One thing is certain: kombucha is a healthy alternative to commercial soft drinks. It's brimming with living organisms and contains only a fraction of the sugar.

If you want to brew kombucha yourself, find out if anyone you know is a brewer and ask them for a piece of their mother scoby to use as a starter. Failing that, buy a bottle of commercially brewed kombucha and pour the contents into an open glass jar. Cover it with (cheese)cloth secured with a rubber band and let it stand at room

temperature. After a while a new scoby will form on top of the liquid and you can then use this for your own brews. Choose a kombucha that has no added flavours or aromas, and make sure you use a live, unpasteurised kombucha as this will contain living organisms.

kombucha   24

BASIC RECIPE

Ingredients for 1 litre:

- 1 kombucha scoby
- 100 ml live kombucha
- 5 g loose leaf black tea (or 3 tea bags)
- 50-100 g unrefined cane sugar (to taste)
- 1 litr ɔltered water

1 glass jɛ (1.5 litre capacity)

METHOD

1. Bring 250 ml water to the boil and use this to make the tea, letting it steep for at least 10 minutes. Add the sugar and stir until it has dissolved. Pour the sweetened tea into the glass jar and add 750 ml cold water.

Because the scoby will not survive temperatures higher than 40°C, it's important to make certain that the liquid is not too hot. Once it has cooled down enough, add the scoby and the 100 ml live kombucha to the liquid. This will increase the acidity of the mixture immediately and create conditions in which the kombucha organisms feel at home. Other, potentially harmful bacteria will not be able to survive in the acidic environment.

2. Cover the jar with (cheese)cloth and secure it with a rubber band. The kombucha needs air to ferment, but the cloth keeps dust and insects out. Leave the liquid to ferment for 7 to 14 days at room temperature in a dark place. Then taste the kombucha. If it's too sweet for you, leave it to ferment more. The longer you wait, the less sugar it will contain.

3. Once the tea is to your liking remove the scoby and 100 ml of the tea from the jar to use for your next brew. Strain the remaining kombucha to remove any bits of scoby before bottling it. Pour the liquid into glass bottles and close them well. Store the bottles at room temperature for a day or two to allow the drink to build up some fizz. Keep an eye on the bottles to make sure the pressure doesn't build up too much. Before that happens, put the bottles in the fridge to stop the fermentation process.

TIPS

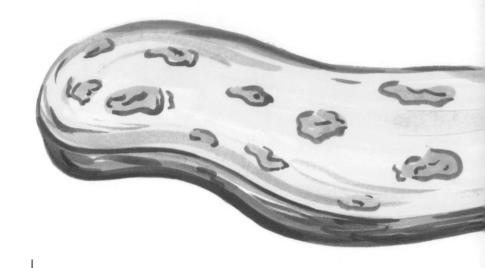

To brew kombucha you need real tea from the tea plant rather than herbal tea. Infusions like camomile or linden blossom won't work. Don't use teas like Earl Grey that contain aromatic oils as these will damage the scoby.

If you don't want to make a new batch immediately, just leave the scoby floating in the kombucha. It will survive like this for a few months until you're ready to start up again.

If the scoby has sunk to the bottom and doesn't rise back to the surface within a couple of hours, sadly this means your scoby has died. You'll have to start again with a new scoby. On the other hand, if the scoby sinks to the bottom but a new layer forms on the surface, there's nothing to worry about. Throw away the piece that has sunk and continue with your new scoby.

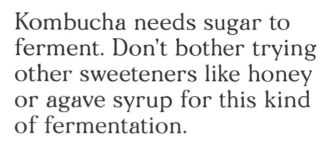

Kombucha needs sugar to ferment. Don't bother trying other sweeteners like honey or agave syrup for this kind of fermentation.

↓

During each round of fermentation, a new, white layer forms on top of the original scoby. After a few rounds of brewing, peel off the older, darker layers and pass them on to someone else who wants to start their own kombucha brew, or chuck them on the compost heap.

↓

Keep a close eye on the kombucha scoby: it mustn't start to smell 'off' and should stay a creamy white colour. Sometimes dark strings of residue from the black tea start to grow on the underside, but these are nothing to worry about. If you think mould is starting to form, though, it's safer to throw scoby and all away and start again.

↓

If you've forgotten about your brew and it has become so sour that it's undrinkable, use the batch as you would wine vinegar — for a vinaigrette or straight on a salad. Alternatively, mix it with fruit juice to sweeten it.

Experiment with herbs and fruit

Once you've completed the first round of fermentation described in the basic recipe, why not try adding flavours during a second fermentation? If so, make sure you stop the first fermentation round while the kombucha still tastes fairly sweet. Even though you don't add a scoby for the second round, the organisms in the kombucha will continue to convert the sugar into acids and bubbles.

Remove the scoby from the kombucha and keep a bit of brewed kombucha aside for your next batch. Pour the rest of the liquid into another glass jar. Add your flavourings and cover the jar with (cheese)cloth. Leave the mixture at room temperature for 2 to 5 days. Once you've got the taste you want, bottle the kombucha.

1. If you're adding flavourings that don't require straining, like fruit juice, you can do the second fermentation in the bottles. Don't forget to open the bottles now and then so the pressure doesn't build up too much.

2. Ideas for flavourings: slices of ginger or turmeric, citrus fruit segments or peel, apple juice, cranberry juice, blueberry juice, beetroot juice, carrot juice and herbs such as verbena, fennel seed, hibiscus, lavender or hops.

3. Combinations that work well: fennel seed with orange segments, hops with a little honey, lavender and lemon peel.

Try out
other teas

Try out different kinds of tea for a change. Green tea will make a refreshing, light kombucha. White tea produces a delicately flavoured kombucha that combines well with other aromatics.

For more robust flavours try using pu-erh tea or smoked tea.

2 WATER KEFIR

The exact origins of kefir remain a mystery. Throughout history, the grains have cropped up in Japan, Tibet, the Caucasus, and Mexico. In 1899, the French scientist Louis Lutz wrote the first scientific report on water kefir after a visit to Mexico, where the kefir grains are called tibicos.

In his *Recherches biologiques sur la constitution du Tibi* he writes: 'The tibicos originated in Mexico, where they grow on the leaves of the Opuntia cactus. When they come into contact with water in which sugar has been dissolved, this leads to a fermentation. The result is a sparkling drink with a sour flavour that is a little buttery. It is mainly drunk by factory workers. The tibicos look like tiny transparent beads, similar to cooked grains of rice'.

Whether the culture really originated in the sweet juice of a cactus plant where a group of yeasts and bacteria began a cosy life together we will never know, but it makes for a good story.

FOR STARTERS

You need a scoby — short for symbiotic culture of bacteria and yeasts — for making water kefir, but this one is completely different from a kombucha scoby. Kefir scoby resembles tiny, transparent grains.

Making water kefir doesn't take long at all. It's ready to drink in no time, so it's the ideal drink for embarking on your adventures in fermentation.

water kefir 40

BASIC RECIPE

Ingredients for 1 litre:

- 2 tbsp water kefir grains
- 50-100 g unrefined cane sugar (to taste)
- 1 litre filtered water
- Juice of 1/2 a lemon or 1/2 a lemon, sliced
- 1 untreated dried fig (optional)

1 glass jar (1.5 litre capacity)

METHOD

1. Mix the sugar with the water in the glass jar. Stir well until the sugar has dissolved. Add the kefir grains, lemon juice or slices, and the fig if you are using it. Cover the jar with (cheese)cloth and secure with a rubber band. Leave to ferment for 48 hours.

2. After 2 days, strain the grains from the liquid. If you wish, start a new batch immediately.

3. Pour the water kefir into glass bottles and close them. Keep the bottles at room temperature for a day or two to allow the drink to become carbonated. Water kefir ferments fast, so make sure you put the bottles in the fridge to stop the fermentation process before the pressure in the bottles builds up so much that they explode.

TIPS

↓

Because kefir brewing is such a quick process, you may start to find it too much to have to start a new batch every two days. If you want to take a break, you can put the grains in a sugar-water solution and keep them in the fridge for about two weeks without having to give them extra food. You can also try freezing kefir grains or drying them and then soaking them to revive them when you need them. Since there is a chance your grains won't survive the process of freezing and drying, don't try this with your only reserves.

↓

Kefir grains multiply each time you brew kefir. If you find you have too many grains, give some away or store them in one of the ways described above.

↓

Since kefir grains can also convert other sweeteners besides sugar, you could add maple syrup, agave, rice or barley malt syrup to the water instead.

↓

You can buy kefir grains online (make sure that you order the type for water kefir and not the ones for fermenting milk) or see if you can find someone in your own circle or through an online forum who has some to give away.

If you want healthy grains that grow vigorously, it's worth adding that fig.

↓

I have had many a heated discussion with my mother about whether you need to add a fig to your kefir or not. She always does. Even though I was the one who introduced her to kefir brewing with a recipe that did not include a fig, she has become so enthusiastic that she started googling. She found many recipes that added a fig, so she did too. Because her kefir grains grow so fast and are glowing with health, I couldn't resist trying to find out what the reason might be. It turns out that figs contain loads of minerals, like calcium, iron, potassium and selenium, and these boost the growth of the kefir grains.

Festive with fruit

Adding extra fruit and aromatics makes for some really delicious water kefir. Try half a grapefruit and five bruised cardamom pods for a refined, delicate pink 'lemonade'. Add half each of a lemon and an orange (sliced) for a citrus tonic. A mandarin orange and a cinnamon stick make for a wintry drink. To avoid the kefir becoming bitter, remove both the zest and the pith of the citrus fruits and use only the flesh. In summer, use strawberries, blueberries, or plums to make fruity sodas.

Remember, kefir grains grow best when you use the basic recipe, so don't use your only supply of kefir grains if you are going to add extra fruit or an infusion.

Try tea instead of water

You can also use a herbal infusion to make water kefir: brew a strong pot of hibiscus, verbena or other herb tea and mix the sugar into it. Make sure the tea has cooled down before you add the grains: they will not survive above 40°C.

Bear in mind: if you use strongly coloured infusions, such as hibiscus, your kefir grains will take on the same colour. That's not a problem though, as the next time you use them they will become colourless again.

Fruit juice does the job

You can also use fruit juice instead of the water in the basic recipe. If you do so, there's no need to add extra sugar as fruit juice already contains enough. You can use juices that are freshly squeezed, bottled, or in cartons. Fermenting apple-cherry juice with kefir grains will give you a tart fizzy drink reminiscent of Belgian Kriek beer. If you have half a watermelon lying around, put it through the juicer and add the kefir grains to the juice to produce a summery delicate pink soda. If you don't have enough juice or the taste is too strong, dilute the juice with sweetened water (use 50-100 g sugar to 1 litre of water).

3   MILK KEFIR

Milk kefir is said to have originated among shepherds in the Caucasus, an area where Europe and Asia meet. The shepherds made kefir by hanging fresh cow's, goat's or sheep's milk in an open leather bag next to the door. Everyone who entered the house was supposed to hit the bag with a stick to help oxygen circulate and thus get the fermentation going. After two days, the milk would turn refreshingly tart and slightly fizzy, earning it the name 'milk champagne'.

According to legend, the people of the Caucasus wanted to keep this special health-giving drink a secret as long as they could. They believed that the milk kefir grains needed to start the fermentation had been given to them by God, through the prophet Mohammed. If the grains became too widely dispersed they would lose their divine power. So, they were carefully guarded and cherished and passed on only from one generation to the next.

The story goes that, in the early 20th century, a Russian woman seduced Prince Bek-Mirza Barchorov and managed to get him to reveal the secret of milk kefir. She had been sent by a Russian doctor who wanted to unravel the mystery of this drink and its medicinal properties. This folk tale is often cited to explain how the popularity of this drink also spread to Russia.

FOR STARTERS

Once ready, milk kefir most resembles a tasty yoghurt drink: refreshing, slightly tart, and fizzy on the tongue. But whereas making yoghurt involves heating the milk and keeping the mixture warm during fermentation, kefir can simply be left to do its thing at room temperature. Milk kefir is made with a scoby (symbiotic culture of bacteria and yeast) that looks like small transparent grains with a gelatinous consistency. Bacteria and yeasts live in and on these grains and together they convert your milk into a refreshingly sour yoghurt-like drink. You may be able to find someone you know who makes milk kefir and can give you a quantity to start with; however, the grains are becoming easier to find in the chilled section of natural food shops and you can also buy dried grains online.

Milk kefir is once more being touted for its health-promoting properties.

Various large-scale scientific studies are investigating its beneficial effects on our digestive system and cholesterol balance as well as its anti-inflammatory and anti-bacterial properties.

milk kefir   56

BASIC RECIPE

Ingredients for 1 litre:

- 1 litre whole milk
- 1-2 teaspoons milk kefir grains

1 glass jar (1.5 litre capacity)

METHOD

1. Put the grains in the glass jar and pour the milk over them.

2. Cover the jar with (cheese)cloth or another thin piece of material and secure with a rubber band. Leave to ferment for 24 hours or until the milk has the consistency of a yoghurt drink.

3. Strain the grains from the liquid. To do this, pour the drink through a coarse sieve and stir gently with a spatula or wooden spoon until all the liquid has dripped through the sieve, leaving the grains behind.

4. Keep the kefir in the fridge in a glass jar with the lid on.

5. If you wish, you can start a new batch of kefir straight away.

TIPS

↓

Although the scobys for milk kefir and water kefir look the same, at the microbiological level, they contain different cultures of bacteria and yeasts so you can't use one instead of the other.

↓

Milk kefir grains love milk that comes from animals. You can use cow's milk, but don't forget that goat's milk and sheep's milk are also perfect for making kefir. Goat's milk produces a slightly thinner kefir than cow's milk. Sheep's milk contains more protein and makes a thicker kefir.

↓

The milk kefir grains are happiest in fresh milk and they don't mind whether it is raw or pasteurised. They are not crazy about long life milk, also called UHT, as it has been heated to an Ultra High Temperature. If you use raw milk, make sure it's as fresh as possible, otherwise too many bacteria will have already developed in the milk and they will compete with the milk kefir bacteria.

↓

If you let the kefir ferment for too long, it will separate into curds (solids) and whey (liquid), which makes it more difficult to strain the kefir grains from the kefir. If this happens, you're more likely to succeed if you shake the kefir well so that the liquid and solids recombine. Try using a sieve and, if this doesn't work, fish the grains out with your — freshly washed — hands.

↓

Non-dairy milk is not easy to ferment with milk kefir grains, as they need lactose to thrive. You can certainly experiment with plant-based milk, but the results may not be consistent. Coconut milk is a good bet. It sometimes takes longer to ferment — you will need 2-3 days to obtain a refreshing drink. Taste it regularly until you are happy with it. After brewing two or three batches of coconut milk kefir you'll need to soak the grains in animal milk again so that they can feed.

↓

If you want to take a break from your brewing rhythm, you can store the grains in their favourite food — milk — in the fridge for up to three weeks. You'll need 1 litre of milk to keep them well nourished for this amount of time.

Milk kefir grains are hungry beasties.

↓

If you need to stop brewing for a longer period of time, try drying the kefir grains by rinsing them and leaving them on a piece of kitchen paper for several days. You will usually be able to revive them later by soaking them in milk again. Since the grains don't always survive being dried, though, don't try this with the only ones you have.

↓

Milk kefir grains multiply (as do water kefir grains) each time you brew kefir.

If you find you have too many grains, give some away or store them in one of the ways described above.

↓

After sieving out the kefir grains and pouring the kefir into a jar and sealing it, you can choose to leave it to ferment longer at room temperature. It will start to carbonate and you will get a slightly fizzy version of the drink. Some people love this; others find it peculiar. Try it for yourself to decide which camp you belong to.

Fermentation, round two

Once you've removed the milk kefir grains from the kefir, you can leave the drink to ferment for a few more hours. Add flavouring when you do this and you have an easy way of making a tasty drink. You could add fruit, like orange segments or berries. Alternatively, additions such as a stick of cinnamon, some cardamom pods, or half a stem of lemongrass all give you delicious flavours that combine well with the tartness of the kefir. A spoonful of cocoa powder or grated coconut is also worth trying.

If you add an ingredient that contains sugar, such as fruit, the fermentation will be livelier and the end product is likely to be extra fizzy. If you're not keen on extra bubbles, stick to herbs and spices or other low-sugar additions so that the kefir doesn't start fizzing more.

Kefir cheese

You may find that your consumption doesn't keep up with the amount of kefir you're producing. Don't worry; it's easy to make it into soft cheese. Just place a piece of (cheese)-cloth in a sieve and put the sieve over a bowl. Pour in the kefir, tie the (cheese)cloth in a knot above the kefir and let the whole thing stand in the fridge for a night. You'll get a soft creamy cheese that you can flavour or eat au naturel on a slice of bread.

For cheese of a firmer consistency, leave the kefir to drain for longer. You can even place a weight on top of the cheese to help the liquid drain off.

4 GINGER BEER

Ginger beer was once a tremendously popular drink. Prompted by the arrival of exotic ginger and sugar from their colonies, brewing ginger beer became all the rage among the Brits in the mid 17th century. The product was such a success that they exported it all over the world. Sturdy stoneware crocks protected both the liquid and the bubbles during the long journey. Brewers' lavish use of sugar and yeast drove the alcohol content up as high as 11%.

By the beginning of the 19th century, nearly every city in England had a ginger beer brewery. Street vendors sold the drink, dispensing it from a mechanical beer tap in a cart drawn by a donkey or pony. From 1855 onwards, British excise laws set a limit of 2% alcohol for ginger beer and the drink also became popular for children. During Prohibition in the United States, from 1920 to 1933, imports from England rose: ginger beer was not only a fine alternative to real beer, it was also an ideal mixer to disguise the bad taste of bootleg alcohol from home stills.

Today, commercial ginger beer is no longer brewed or fermented: it is just a soft drink made from water, ginger, sugar, and carbon dioxide (CO_2). This means that now the only difference between ginger beer and ginger ale is that ginger beer has more of a tang because it contains more ginger. In this chapter, we return to its roots with a fermented version.

FOR STARTERS

Fermented ginger beer is a refreshing, fizzy soft drink; despite its name, our recipe has nothing to do with beer. Its very low alcohol content of less than 0.5% puts ginger beer, along with other fermented beverages in this book, in the category of non-alcoholic drinks in most countries. To brew this drink you simply use a starter to add life to a strong, sweetened infusion of ginger. The starter is easy to make yourself from ginger, water and sugar. You feed the mixture every day — as you would a sourdough starter — until it begins to bubble. As easy as making ginger beer is, though, it does involve quite a lot of effort, so the recipe below yields a large quantity at once.

Still, we suspect that once you have tasted your own home-brewed ginger beer you will soon want to start up a new batch.

ginger beer   72

BASIC RECIPE

Ingredients for 8 litres:

For the starter:

- 150 g organic ginger
- 5 tbsp unrefined cane sugar
- 800 ml filtered water

For the ginger tea:

- 250 g organic ginger
- 8 litres filtered water
- 400-800 g unrefined cane sugar (to taste)
- Juice of 4 lemons

1 glass jar (1 litre capacity)

1 glass container (10 litre capacity, of the demijohn/carboy type)

METHOD

1. Make a starter by mixing 2 tablespoons of coarsely
    grated ginger with 2 tablespoons of sugar and 800 ml
    of water in a glass jar. Stir well with a wooden spoon.
    Put the starter in a warm place and stir frequently.
    Every day add 1 tablespoon grated ginger and 1 table-
    spoon sugar until the starter starts to fizz. The process
    may take only a couple of days but sometimes you
    have to be more patient.

2. Once your starter is showing signs of life, make the ginger tea. Slice the ginger finely, add it to 4 litres of the filtered water and boil, covered, for 15 minutes. Add the sugar and stir well. Dilute the strong ginger tea with the remaining 4 litres of filtered water so that the liquid cools more quickly. Let it cool to body temperature. Transfer the tea into the large glass container.

3. Once the tea is cool enough — waiting is essential because adding the starter when the liquid is too warm would mean sudden death for the carefully cultured organisms — strain the starter to remove the ginger pieces and add the liquid to the tea. Add the lemon juice and allow your brew to continue fermenting at room temperature in the large glass container. Cover the opening with a thin (cheese)cloth secured with a rubber band or with an airlock. Swill the liquid in the container occasionally to aerate the mixture. When it

starts to fizz, usually after about 3 days, your ginger beer is ready for bottling. Since this process can take a longer or shorter time, depending on the temperature, let your taste buds help you decide when to bottle.

4. Pour the ginger beer into glass bottles and seal them. Leave the bottles at room temperature for a day or two so that the drinks can become carbonated, but put the bottles in the fridge before the pressure in the bottles increases too much.

TIPS

↓
It's best to use organic ginger, peel and all, since that peel contains the most yeasts that will give your brew a flying start.

↓
You can also make the starter from fresh turmeric root. Adding it to your ginger beer gives you a magnificent orange drink with a fruity turmeric note.

Turmeric boost

Jamu is a herbal drink consumed as a health tonic in Indonesia. Its main ingredient is turmeric. For a fermented version of jamu, substitute turmeric for half of the ginger in the ginger tea in the basic recipe and add 2 tablespoons of tamarind pulp when you boil it. Allow it to cool off and then add some freshly ground black pepper and the juice of 4 limes. After that, continue to follow the steps in the basic recipe.

Feeling adventurous?
Give roots a whirl

Root beer is a remarkable drink. It is dark, aromatic stuff —
though commercial root beer also tends to be extremely
sweet. This is your chance to brew a healthy, refreshing
version. Its dark brown colour comes from a strong infusion made with tree roots and bark such as liquorice
root, sassafras, sarsaparilla, or dandelion and burdock. In
fact, you can use all kinds of roots and concoct your own
mix. Liquorice root, for instance, considered essential by
most root beer aficionados, is one I don't use because the
flavour is too strong for my taste. Feel free to experiment
with any edible roots and bark you can find. Make a strong
infusion with them instead of ginger and continue as described in the basic recipe.

Your own Orangina

While you might think it's asking for trouble to keep fresh fruit juice at room temperature, fear not! The bacteria in the ginger starter will turn it into a delicious, sparkling soft drink. You don't need to add extra sugar because the juice itself contains enough for fermentation.

Ingredients for 1 litre:
- 800 ml freshly squeezed orange juice
- 200 ml ginger starter (see basic recipe)

Method:
- Mix the orange juice with the ginger starter.
- Let the orange juice ferment in a jar at room temperature. Stir every now and then. It is ready for bottling when it starts to fizz, usually after about 3 days. It can take a longer or shorter time depending on the temperature. Taste it regularly and when it's to your liking, bottle the liquid.
- Strain the juice, pour into glass bottles and seal them. Leave the bottles at room temperature for no more than 12 hours — even less if it's warm, since this drink carbonates very quickly and can otherwise lead to explosive drama. Put the bottles in the fridge before that happens.

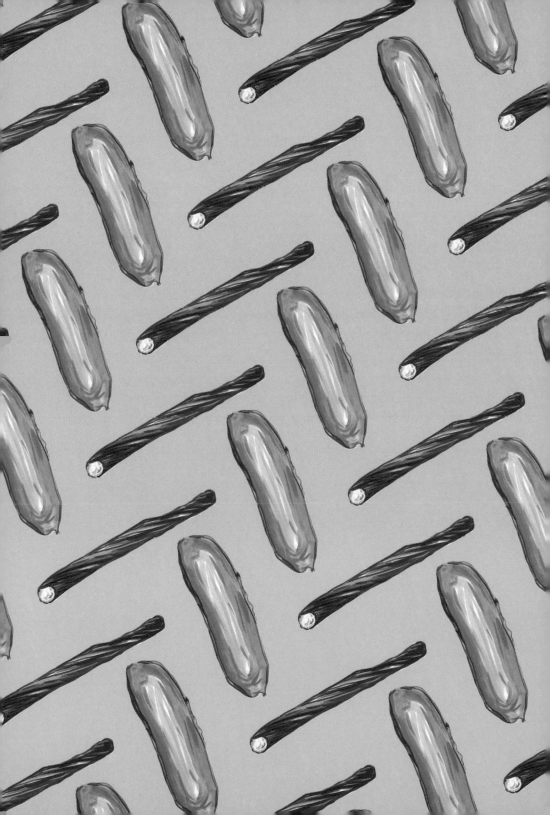

5 BREAD KVASS

Kvass is a fermented drink made from old rye bread. In the traditional Slavic recipe, stale bread was soaked in water and wild yeasts in the air brought the mixture to life. After it had fermented for a few days, people drank the whole lot — bread and all — so as not to lose any of the goodness. More recent versions strain the bread out of the drink and they no longer rely solely on wild yeasts; instead they use baker's or brewer's yeast or sourdough as a starter. Kvass is enormously popular in Russia and surrounding countries: it is the authentic soft drink of the region.

Kvass has been brewed commercially since the 19th century and fruit and herbal versions are available too. There are still plenty of commercial kvass breweries in Russia. In fact, kvass has even acquired political overtones: one of the big Russian kvass brands launched a campaign urging 'anti-cola-nisation', promoting kvass as a healthy and patriotic alternative to the soft drinks produced by big multinationals.

FOR STARTERS

Kvass is a refreshing drink with a distinct grain flavour. In the summer, it's like a refreshing beer minus the alcohol. Making kvass is a wonderful way to use up old bread.

If the taste is a little too strong for you, do try the recipe using apple juice for a delicious, mellower alternative.

bread kvass   86

BASIC RECIPE

Ingredients for 1 litre:

- 75 g (dry) dark bread
- 1.5 litres water
- Pinch of salt
- 50-100 g sugar
  (to taste)
- Juice of 1/4 lemon
- 1 tbsp sourdough starter or
  1 tsp baker's or brewer's yeast

1 glass jar (1.5 litre capacity)

METHOD

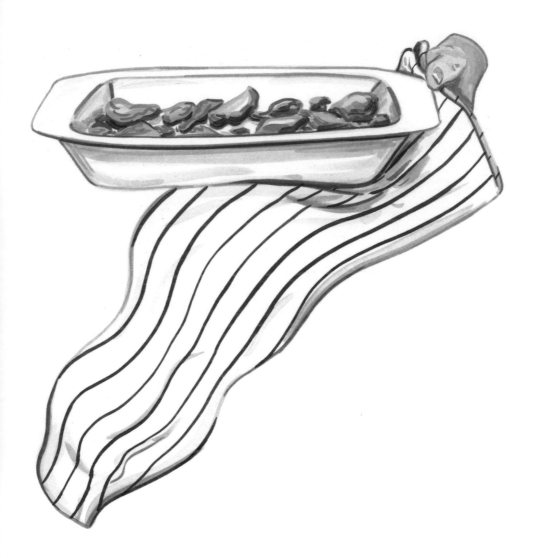

1.   Toast the bread in a hot oven or in a toaster until it is
     dark brown. This will give the drink an attractive dark
     colour and a lightly roasted flavour.

2. Bring the water to the boil. Put the toasted bread in a cooking pot and pour the water over it. Cover the pot and let the mixture steep overnight.

3. Pour the liquid through a sieve into the glass jar, pressing the liquid out of the bread in the sieve to extract as much kvass as possible. Add the sugar, lemon juice, and sourdough starter or yeast to the liquid and leave it to ferment for 48 hours or until foam forms on the surface.

bread kvass   90

4. Pour the kvass into glass bottles. Leave the sediment behind in the glass jar; it contains the dead yeast cells and these won't do your final product any good. Close the bottles and keep them at room temperature for a day or two to allow the drink to carbonate. Keep an eye on the bottles and make sure you put them in the fridge before the pressure builds up too much.

TIPS

If you want a kvass that's even more beer-like, add some dried hops for that bitter taste.

↓

Traditionally, mint is added to kvass as a flavouring. Other herbs such as thyme and rosemary are also popular. Add about 1 teaspoon of dried herbs to the hot water together with the bread.

↓

Raisins add a fruity note. Try adding a tablespoon of raisins to the bread and hot water.

↓

If you like the result and make kvass regularly, you can omit the yeast or sourdough and use a little of the previous batch of kvass as a starter for your next fermentation.

↓

Traditionally rye bread is used, but other dark bread or sourdough works fine.

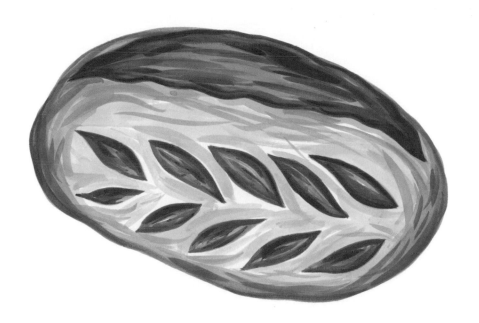

Mix apple juice with sourdough bread

I was given this recipe by sommelier Taike Verdonck. I was blown away by her non-alcoholic drink pairing during a meal at the exceptional restaurant of Belgian chef, Kobe Desramaults. Verdonck excels at building delicate layers of taste by mixing drinks that contain vegetable and fruit juices, fermented tea, infusions, and herbs.

     The fresh notes and light texture of her non-alcoholic accompaniments are every bit as good as the wine pairings. I am delighted that she has allowed me to share her recipe for this wonderful digestif.

The bread lends creaminess to the apple juice, and the warming spices are a perfect way to end a meal.

Ingredients:

- 750 ml apple juice (fresh or bottled)
- 200 g sourdough bread cut in pieces
- 2 cinnamon sticks
- 2 star anise
- 1 tsp brown sugar or Sirop de Liège

Method:

Mix all the ingredients and leave them to ferment for 5 days in a sealed container. Once a day, stir the mixture with a wooden spoon. Filter the spices out and pour the liquid into a glass bottle. Leave it at room temperature for another 2 days to develop some fizz. After that, keep it in the fridge.

6 WHEY KVASS

The bread-based drink described in the previous chapter became so popular in the Slavic and Baltic countries that people started to use the name 'kvass' for other tart drinks too. One of these was a fermented favourite made with beetroot. Although the drinks have a common name and come from the same region, they are made in very different ways. For this reason I have devoted a chapter to each kvass.

In Poland, beet kvass is used to give the traditional beetroot soup (barszcz) its typically sour taste. You can buy bottles of the stuff in shops, but many people brew it themselves at home as it's easy to make and keeps well. In Ukraine, aficionados swear by a shot on an empty stomach as the best way to achieve the maximum purifying effect.

FOR STARTERS

This ruby red drink is regarded as a true health tonic. Beetroots themselves have the reputation of being a superfood. They contain nutrients such as folic acid, potassium, iron and magnesium and their red pigments are powerful antioxidants. And to top it off, the lactic acid bacteria in the whey make this drink a probiotic booster. Beet kvass contains no added sugar. It's made simply from water, a pinch of salt and chunks of beetroot.

It is the ideal recipe for anyone who prefers savoury to sweet drinks. You can make it even more aromatic by adding extra flavourings.

It's possible to make beet kvass without using a starter, relying purely on the wild yeasts in the air and on the beetroot peel, but we like the results we get from adding a little whey: a cleaner and more complex flavour.

Whey is the liquid produced when rennet is added to milk or when milk is allowed to ferment spontaneously: the milk separates into solids (curds) and liquid (whey). Whey from raw (unpasteurised) or fermented milk is brimming with bacteria that produce lactic acid. The easiest way to get hold of whey at home is to drain the liquid from yoghurt. Line a sieve with (cheese)cloth

and place the sieve over a bowl, or even easier, use a coffee filter on top of a cup. If you have some milk kefir on hand, you can let it ferment for longer than you usually would, until it separates into solids and liquid. Whey from yoghurt or kefir contains masses of lactobacilli, which will give your fermenting kvass a flying start.

whey kvass 100

BASIC RECIPE

Ingredients for 1 litre:

- 350 g whole beetroot
- 1 litre filtered water
- 1 tsp salt
- 2 tbsp whey

1 glass jar (1.5 litre capacity)

METHOD

1. Carefully rinse any soil off the beetroot, but don't scrub them completely clean: the bacteria on the skin help to get fermentation going.

2. Cut the beetroot (do not peel!) into small chunks. In the glass jar, mix the salt and whey into the water and add the chunks of beetroot. Cover with (cheese)cloth, secure with a rubber band and leave to ferment at room temperature until the mixture develops a gentle fizz.

3. Stir well once a day so that the beetroot that is in contact with the air doesn't start to moulder. The fermentation process can take anywhere from 3 days to 2 weeks, depending on the temperature. Taste every day until the kvass has a pleasant, refreshing flavour.

whey kvass   104

4. Strain the liquid to remove the chunks and pour the kvass into bottles. Let these stand at room temperature for another 24 hours to build up the bubbles in the bottles. After that keep them in the fridge.

TIPS

Add a little ginger for kvass with more punch. Herbs like caraway or thyme will give it a more savoury taste.

↓

Don't use whey that is a by-product of cheesemaking, as this has been heated during the process and no longer contains any living microbes.

↓

Don't be tempted to grate the beetroot instead of dicing it. Grated beetroot releases too much juice. The natural sugars in the juice speed up the fermentation so much that alcohol is produced instead of lactic acid.

↓

The beetroot chunks left after straining the kvass are actually lacto-fermented vegetables. Don't throw them away; instead use them in soups, juices, or salads.

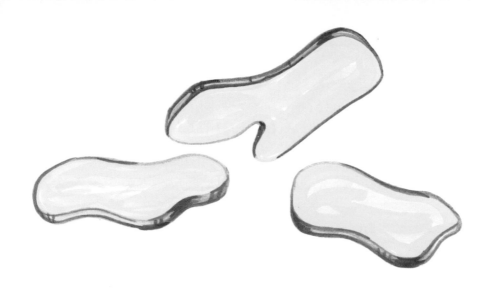

Swap beetroot for carrot

Here's an ideal variation for anyone who isn't keen on the earthiness of beetroot: substitute an equal amount of finely chopped carrot for the beetroot in the basic recipe. Add the peel of 1 orange and a couple of slices of ginger

Fruitful variations

Try a similar amount of fruit instead of the beetroot in the basic recipe. Your best bet is to use fruit that releases its juice easily, like citrus fruit or berries. Bruise the berries gently; cut citrus fruit into slices and — if you're after a slightly bitter taste — use the peel as well. Fruity variations make for great drinks with no added sugar.

Hibiscus soda

Perhaps we're stretching it a bit far to call this drink a kvass — especially as it contains added sugar — but because we do use whey as a starter, we've included this stray recipe in the chapter.

Ingredients for 1 litre:

- 1 litre water
- 10 g dried hibiscus flowers
- Juice of 1 lemon
- 50-100 g sugar (to taste)
- 2 tbsp whey

Method:

1. Bring the water to the boil. Add the hibiscus flowers and lower the heat to let the mixture simmer gently for 5 minutes.

2. Add the sugar, stir, and let the mixture cool.

3. Pour the sweetened infusion through a sieve to remove the flowers. Put the liquid and the whey into a glass jar. Cover with (cheese)cloth, secure with a rubber band and leave to ferment at room temperature until the mixture starts to fizz. Help the process along by stirring the mixture well once a day.

4. Once the mixture is bubbly, let it ferment for another 2 days until you have the taste you like. The longer you wait, the more tart and less sweet the flavour will become. Pour into bottles and let these stand at room temperature for another 24 hours to build up the bubbles. After that keep them in the fridge.

7 MEAD

Mead, a mythic drink brewed simply from honey, water, and wild or cultured yeasts, goes back even further in history than wine: it is thought to be the oldest alcoholic drink in the world.

The ancient Greeks even called it the nectar of the gods. In Greek mythology, king of the gods Zeus used mead to get his father, Cronus, drunk. In India, ancient Hindu texts refer to it and, in Central Africa, honey wine, called t'ej, is still being consumed to this day. The Egyptians were ardent brewers too, and mead was found in the tombs of the pharaohs. We also know it as the drink that Gauls and Teutons gulped down from cow horns before facing battle.

FOR STARTERS

In its original form, mead is honey wine. But as we are exploring non-alcoholic drinks in this book, we use more water and less honey. Since less honey means less sugar for the yeasts to turn into alcohol, the result is not a wine but a sparkling honey drink. After a brief fermentation, put the mead in the fridge to stop the process.

When you drink this young mead, you taste the honey's floral bouquet without its typically overpowering sweetness. It's easy to make young mead, and you are likely to have the ingredients for it in your kitchen cupboard at this very moment.

mead   114

BASIC RECIPE

Ingredients for 1 litre:

- 1 litre water
- 150 g cold-extracted honey

1 glass jar (1.5 litre capacity)

METHOD

1. Mix the water and honey and give it a good stir. Don't worry if the honey doesn't dissolve right away: in time, the two elements will blend. Cover the jar with a thin (cheese)cloth secured with a rubber band.

2. Let the mixture ferment at room temperature, stirring it once a day.

3. After about 5 days — less if it is warm — you will have a slightly fizzy drink.

4. Pour the mead into glass bottles and close them. Let carbonation develop at room temperature for another day, but keep an eye on the bottles to make sure the pressure doesn't build up too much. Before that happens put the bottles in the fridge.

TIPS

↓

Be aware of where your honey comes from. Every region has its own regulations about honey. For instance, the European Union does not allow sugar to be mixed into honey in order to increase its volume but, in some other regions, the rules are different. Look for pure honey that has not been diluted. The best source is a local beekeeper, who will have honey produced from flowers and plants nearby. This will give you a uniquely local product, alive with organisms from your own environment.

↓

Use cold-extracted or raw honey, since honey which has not been heated still contains all of its living yeasts. In the honeypot, the high sugar concentration keeps anything from happening, but the yeasts become active as soon as you add water. Nothing, however, can revive the wild yeasts in heat-processed honey.

Trust your sense of taste for when to bottle it: it's ready when you're happy with it!

↓

Do you want to try making honey wine? The principle is the same, but you use more honey. A ratio of 1 part honey to 2 parts water works well. If you want to drink the mead young, bottle it after 2 weeks, which is the point when the mead stops producing bubbles. You can also let the mead ferment longer, up to a few months. If you want to try that, transfer the mead after the first 2 weeks of fermentation into a glass container with a slender neck (a demijohn or carboy). Leave the sediment behind, as it only contains dead yeast cells that won't improve the taste of your end product. Make sure you fill the demijohn all the way to the neck: the whole idea of the shape of these containers is to minimise contact between the fluid and the air. Since vinegar bacteria need oxygen to turn alcohol to acetic acid, limiting contact with the air will lower the risk of spoiling your wine. Let the mead ferment for a number of weeks or months.

Even more flowers

To make your mead even more flowery, add a tablespoon of dried lavender flowers, rosebuds or chamomile to the water/honey mix and let them infuse in the fermenting liquid. Strain the liquid to remove the blooms before you bottle the mead.

Juicy berries

Juicy summer fruit yields a distinctive mead. Flavour it with strawberries, blackberries, or redcurrants. If it's warm, make sure that you strain off the liquid after 2 days so the mead can go on fermenting without the fruit. Otherwise, because the fruit floats, its contact with the air could cause it to moulder.

Spice up your mead

Combine fruit with tea or spices for more complex flavours. A particularly delicious combination is mead with the rind of an orange and a tablespoon of rooibos tea.

8   TEPACHE

For centuries, Mexico has been a paradise for anyone who likes fermented drinks. Pulque is made from fermented agave juice and tejuino and pozol from the dough used to make corn tortillas and tamales. But the most popular drink by far is tepache, which was initially also made from maize.

In fact, the name tepache comes from tepiātl, a Nahuatl word meaning 'drink made from maize'. The Nahua, the original inhabitants of Central Mexico, were already brewing this fermented soft drink in pre-Hispanic times.

Later, the maize was replaced by fruits such as pineapple, apple, and orange. The fruit rind and pulp ferment in water with brown sugar and seasonings, traditionally in a wooden cask. To this day, tepache is very popular in Mexico, sold there by street vendors, and its alcohol content is regularly given a boost by mixing it with beer.

FOR STARTERS

For the basic recipe I chose a version using apple, a fruit plentiful in our temperate part of the world. Of course, you can also make the popular version with pineapple: you'll find that recipe further on. It's ideal to start this apple tepache when you are making apple sauce or apple pie.

The peel and cores that you would normally throw away get a second life as a fragrant soft drink.

tepache   126

BASIC RECIPE

Ingredients for 1 litre:

- Peel and cores from 5 apples
- 100 g brown sugar
- 2 star anise
- 3 cloves
- 1 cinnamon stick
- 2 slices of lemon
- 1300 ml filtered water

A 1.5 litre preserving jar with a lid

METHOD

1. Put all the ingredients in a preserving jar that you can
    close. Shake the jar until the sugar dissolves. Bruise
    the apple peels a little with a potato masher or wooden
    spoon so that they release more juice.

2. Close the jar and allow it to ferment in a warm place. Once a day, shake the jar well and then open it briefly to release the pressure.

3. After 2-3 days your tepache should taste refreshing and aromatic.

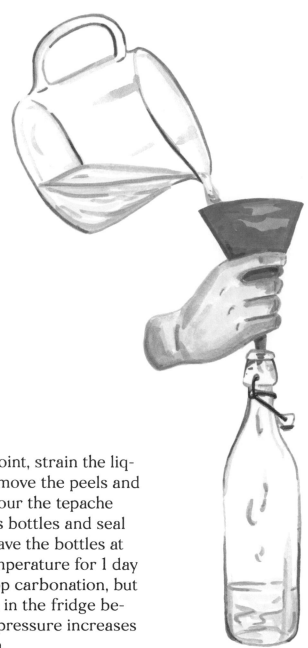

4. At that point, strain the liquid to remove the peels and spices, pour the tepache into glass bottles and seal them. Leave the bottles at room temperature for 1 day to develop carbonation, but put them in the fridge before the pressure increases too much.

TIPS

Tepache evolves quickly, even when refrigerated. It's best to use it up within a week.

↓

If you leave your tepache to ferment for too long it will start to taste like vinegar. Don't pour it down the drain in disappointment, just let it ferment some more in an open glass jar covered with a thin (cheese)cloth secured by a rubber band. You'll end up with a perfectly usable apple cider vinegar.

↓

For a more intense taste you can use panela instead of brown sugar. These hard chunks of unrefined sugar are made from pure cane sugar, which has been boiled and evaporated. Because nothing has been filtered out of the juice, it adds intense smoky and caramelised flavours.

I (heart) pineapple

For a delicately smoky and extremely refreshing drink, swap the apple peels for the rind and heart of a pineapple.

Go full orange!

Try a version with orange for a change. Make sure to get untreated oranges for this experiment, as you will use both the peel and the flesh for delicious results. Note that the peels alone would produce a bitter drink and they have too little sugar for fermentation. With just 2 oranges per litre you will get a truly fruity drink.

9 COCKTAILS

The refreshing acidity of fermented drinks makes them a perfect ingredient for cocktails. Simply add a shot of your favourite alcoholic drink to your glass of water kefir, kombucha, beet kvass, or ginger beer and voila! — you have an elegant long drink in your hands. Ideal for when guests drop in or for moments when you are in need of something a little stronger.

In this chapter, we give you some extra ideas to bring out your inner mixologist as you experiment with your new collection of fermented brews. Let's just call it retox after detox.

Red Devil

This cocktail saw the light of day during the World Cup. Its red colour made it the perfect drink for supporters of the Belgian football team, the Red Devils. Earthy kvass teams up with an aromatic syrup in this cocktail. Together they make a superb thirst-quenching long drink.

Ingredients for the cocktail:

- 50 ml beet kvass
- 30 ml vodka
- 30 ml lemon juice
- 30 ml tarragon syrup

TIP: Not keen on tarragon? Use dill instead.

For the syrup:

- 250 ml water
- 125 g sugar
- 2 tbsp dried tarragon

Method:

Start the tarragon syrup by putting the water and sugar in a saucepan and bringing them to the boil. Add the dried tarragon, turn the heat down and let the mixture simmer gently for 5 minutes. Remove from the heat, let the syrup cool down and then strain it to remove the tarragon.

Make the cocktail by mixing all the ingredients in a cocktail shaker, and then pour into a tall glass filled with ice.

Calpis-Sake

Calpis is a fizzy soft drink that is popular in Japan. It's usually made of fermented milk — but — it turns out you can make a great Calpis with milk kefir. Don't be put off by the sound of it. The moment your lips touch the glass, you'll discover how delicious and refreshing it is. Add sake to make a Japanese-inspired milky white cocktail.

Ingredients for the cocktail:

- 50 ml milk kefir syrup
- 50 ml sake
- 150 ml sparkling water
- 1 slice of lemon

For the syrup:

- 250 ml milk kefir
- 200 g sugar
- 70 ml lemon juice
- Few drops of vanilla essence

Method:

Make the syrup by placing the milk kefir and the sugar in a heatproof bowl. Bring about 5 cm of water to a simmer in a saucepan and place the bowl over the top, making sure the bottom of the bowl doesn't touch the water. Whisk the mixture continuously until the sugar has dissolved completely and it has a reached a temperature of about 70°C. Let the mixture cool. Once it has cooled stir in the lemon juice and vanilla essence. Pour into a clean bottle and keep in the fridge. The syrup will keep for a few weeks.

To make the cocktail, mix the syrup and the sake in a tall glass and top up with sparkling water. Give it a quick stir and serve with a slice of lemon.

Kombucha rhubarb cocktail

This thirst-quenching cocktail is a drink that's hard to put down. The rhubarb adds extra fruity tartness to your kombucha and is balanced by the sweetness of the apple.

Ingredients:

- 50 ml gin
- 100 ml apple & rhubarb juice
- 100 ml kombucha

Method:

Mix all the ingredients in a cocktail shaker, and then serve on the rocks in a tall glass.

ABOUT

Our first encounter with each other was in an Amsterdam basement apartment, while slightly tipsy. The cellar was the setting for an improvised dinner with sausages, wine, and pickles and organised by mutual friends. At the end of the evening, two young women in the assembled company started arm wrestling. That was us. This book is the direct result of that showdown. Our next encounter didn't take place until five years later, at an initial meeting for this project. In the meantime, however, we had kept a watchful eye on each other, and our wish to meld text and illustrations in a culinary project grew stronger. The result is Fizz.

We hope it's to your taste.

Elise van Iterson lives in Amsterdam where she has worked for more than ten years as an illustrator and chef.

She has illustrated for various magazines and newspapers, including *Vrij Nederland, ELLE Eten, NRC Handelsblad* and *De Morgen*. With author Erik Jan Harmens, she created the children's book *Hans is kwijt* (Hans is gone). In addition, she has illustrated a self-published collection of stories and essays, *De Amsterdamse Culinaire Verjaardagskalender* (The Amsterdam Culinary Birthday Calendar), and designed posters and logos for restaurants and events.

As a chef she has worked in restaurants such as Marius/ Worst, Choux and Aan de Amstel.

Barbara Serulus lives in Antwerp and is a food journalist for the Belgian newspaper *De Standaard* and the weekly magazine *Knack Weekend*.

She is also a chef, developer of recipes and co-founder of the culinary project bureau Alle Dagen Honger (Hungry Every Day). As part of Alle Dagen Honger, she organised the food festival Krachtvoer, created a book showcasing the stories of exceptional artisans, *De Helden van het Echte Eten* (The Heroes of Real Food, published by Luster), and has collaborated with many inspiring chefs, farmers, scientists, and designers.

Text: Barbara Serulus
Image: Elise van Iterson
Design: Stef Cuypers
Editor: Jodi van Oudheusden-Peita
Translation: Diane Schaap & Sara Butler

Special thanks to Ad van Iterson for his
help with the translation of this book.

BIS Publishers
Building Het Sieraad
Postjesweg 1
1057 DT Amsterdam
The Netherlands
T   +31(0)20 515 02 30
M   bis@bispublishers.com
W   www.bispublishers.com
ISBN   978-90-6369-544-6
©   2019 Barbara Serulus, Elise van Iterson
         & BIS Publishers.